I0102244

Saviours or Destroyers

The relationship between the human species and the rest of life on Earth

Neil Paul Cummins

Copyright © 2012 by Neil Paul Cummins

All rights reserved. This book, or parts thereof, may not be reproduced in any form without permission.

A catalogue record for this book is available from the British Library

ISBN: 978-1-907962-52-3

Published by Cranmore Publications

www.cranmorepublications.co.uk

For Nancy

Contents

Preface

There are many ways in which humans can conceptualise the relationship between their species and their surroundings; these 'surroundings' can be taken to be the rest of the life-forms which exist on the Earth, or everything non-human that exists in the universe. In this book I focus on various possible relationships between the human species and the rest of the life-forms that exist (and those that have existed, and those that will exist in the future) on the Earth. Is there no deeply significant and meaningful relationship? Or, is the human species superior in some way? Or, is the human species inferior in some way?

If you are familiar with my previous work you will be aware that I am particularly interested in how the relationship we are exploring relates to the 'environmental crisis'. I have suggested that the human species is superior in some way, and that the environmental crisis/human-induced global warming are positive events which indicate that the human species is fulfilling its role as saviour of life on Earth.

I take this book to be a valuable addition to my previous writings. In it I consider at length the opposing view that the human species is an 'inferior destroyer' of the rest of life on Earth. I also outline the whole range of ways in which it is obvious that technology is in the interests of life on Earth. I also develop the view that the universe is a 'feeling universe' whose movements/evolution is directed by all parts of the universe seeking to move to higher states of feeling; and I explore how this plays out in the day-to-day lives of individual humans as they seek to live more happy and fulfilling lives. Furthermore, I describe how we live in an epoch which can best be described as a 'birthing process'; life on Earth is bringing forth the technological armour which will ensure its future survival. This is a birthing process, which like almost all births, entails a lot of pain and suffering. I suggest that this process will come to an end when the temperature of the atmosphere is being successfully technologically regulated. Finally, I outline the serious environmental problems that we face on the surface of the Earth and urge that we take both technological and non-technological actions to address these problems. If we can successfully do this then we can forge a sustainable and harmonious future for all life on Earth.

Introduction

The aim of this book is to consider the relationship that exists between the human species and the rest of life on Earth. There seem to be three potential views which one can have:

1 There is no deeply significant and meaningful relationship between the human species and the rest of life on Earth.

2 The human species is related to the rest of life on Earth through its superiority. There is a hierarchy of life and the human species is

located at its zenith. The human species is the most precious/valuable/important part of life on Earth.

3 The human species is related to the rest of life on Earth through its inferiority. As the destroyer of a multitude of other life-forms, as the coloniser of the planet, as the destroyer of ecosystems and habitats, as the bringer forth of another mass extinction of life on Earth, the human species must be seen as inferior to all other life-forms. The human species is a 'parasite' which the rest of life on Earth would be far better off without.

I have described the first view as there being no "deeply significant and meaningful relationship"; there is obviously a relationship *of some kind* between the human species and the rest of life on Earth. After all, according to the most widely accepted view, the human species evolved from other life-forms that existed on the Earth, and *it is undoubtedly* currently embedded in a plethora of interrelationships with other planetary life-forms.

Sometimes the human species gains from its relationships with other planetary life-forms; humans use other life-forms for agricultural work, for food, for medicine, for companionship, for entertainment and for education. However, sometimes it is the non-human life-forms which gain from such relationships; when the human species creates new habitats – from cities to farmland – this creates the possibility for certain species to thrive, to greatly expand their population. Furthermore, when the human species introduces an 'alien' (non-native) species to an existing habitat this can also enable the 'alien' life-form to thrive as it overruns the native species which was not prepared for its surprising arrival.

The purpose of the previous paragraph is to highlight that there are a great number of diverse relationships between the human species and the rest of life on Earth, and that some of these relationships are positive for some of these non-human life-forms, whilst some of these relationships are negative for some of these non-human life-forms. Of this there is no doubt. When one analyses the web of human/non-human relationships, there will be a group of non-human life-forms which gain and a group which loose.

Our preceding consideration of the web of human/non-human relationships can be thought of in two different ways. When one considers the group of non-human life-forms that either gain or lose from their relationships with the human species, then one can focus either on 'individual organisms' or on 'species'. Let us start with 'species'. One can say, in general terms, that the 'rat species' has greatly expanded its population size, and is positively thriving, due to the nature of its relationship with the human species. At the other extreme, there are many species which have been driven to extinction because of their relationships with the human species.

The alternative way of thinking about the web of human/non-human relationships is to consider not 'species' but 'individual organisms'. If one takes this approach then one will be dividing all of the individual organisms on the Earth which have a relationship with the human species into two groups – the 'gainers' and the 'losers'. So, Rat A is a gainer, as it is constantly feeding on the waste left by humans; whilst, Rat B is a loser because it was killed in a human-made 'rat-trap'. And, Cat A is a gainer because it is lovingly cared for and fed by humans; whist, Cat B is a loser because it was killed when it was squashed by a human-driven automobile.

There is an important point which arises from the preceding discussion. If one *solely* looks at the relationship between the human species and the rest of life on Earth in this way – by balancing those individual life-forms which gain against those which lose, or by balancing those species which gain against those which lose, then, I suggest, there is no deeply significant and meaningful relationship between the human species and the rest of life on Earth. There will simply be a relationship, which, when the 'positive effects' have been balanced against the 'negative effects' could turn out to be either a beneficial or a harmful relationship (for non-human life-forms) overall.

That this balancing of 'positive' against 'negative' cannot give rise to a deeply significant and meaningful relationship is clear because the outcome of the 'balancing' could change over time. After one has summed up all of the 'positive effects' and balanced them against the 'negative effects' (either for 'species' or 'individual organisms'), then it could turn out that the overall relationship was a 'positive' one for non-human life-forms in the 17th century and a 'negative' one in the 20th century. If there is a deeply significant and meaningful relationship then it will not change over time. The human species will simply either be 'superior' or 'inferior'.[1]

The view that the human species *does not have* a deeply significant and meaningful relationship with the rest of life on Earth (and also with the wider

---

[1] This raises the question of what, exactly, the 'human species' is. Some philosophers believe that all 'species' boundaries arise from human-created conceptualisations. If this is so, this means that 'species' boundaries have many possible locations, or even that there are *not really* any species. Throughout *"An Evolutionary Perspective on the Relationship Between Humans and Their Surroundings: Geoengineering, the Purpose of Life & the Nature of the Universe"* I develop a particular view of what the 'human species' is.

cosmos) is seemingly nicely exemplified in the following assertion by Stephen Hawking:

We are just an advanced breed of monkeys on a minor planet of a very average star[2]

It seems obvious to me that there is a deeply significant and meaningful relationship between the human species and the rest of life on Earth. So, I obviously disagree with anyone who does not believe that this relationship – either of 'superiority' or 'inferiority' – exists. If there is a deeply significant and meaningful relationship between the human species and the rest of life on Earth, then the human species *is not just* "an advanced breed of monkeys".

---

[2] *Der Spiegel* (17 October 1988).

If such a deeply significant and meaningful relationship exists then, in accordance with the second and third views outlined above, the human species is either 'superior' or 'inferior' to the rest of life on Earth. If this is so, it also means that, in contrast to carrying out a 'balancing equation' between those 'species' or 'individual organisms' which gain and those which lose, we need to start thinking in terms of the 'totality of non-human life on the Earth'. In other words, we are not interested in the nature of the relationship between the human species and particular non-human species, or between the human species and individual non-human life-forms; we are interested in the nature of the relationship between the human species and the *totality of non-human Earthly life.* Is the human species 'superior' or 'inferior' to such a totality?

Can you picture this 'totality' in your mind? It might be useful to consider what I say about the nature of 'planetary life' in *Is the Human Species Special?: Why human-induced global warming could be in the interests of life?* (2010, pp. 42-3). It should be kept in mind that what we are interested in here is the 'totality of *non-human* Earthly life'; 'planetary life' is a slightly wider category which also includes humans:

> I should make it clear what I mean by 'plane-tary life'. The phrase does *not* refer to *individual* life-forms; rather, it refers to the *totality* of life-forms that exist on the Earth at a particular moment in time. So, if when one reads the phrase 'planetary life' one thinks of a

particular cat, or a species of cats, then one has missed the meaning that the phrase is meant to convey. One should not even think of 'planetary life' as a *collection of individual* life-forms; one should think of it as *a single entity* that is constituted out of individual life-forms. It is perhaps helpful to imagine that the Earth is divided into two parts – you can imagine that all planetary life-forms are coloured green, whilst all non-living parts of the planet are coloured red; the green part will be 'planetary life'. I will also sometimes use the phrase 'life' to refer to the *totality* of life-forms in the universe; 'life' will be equivalent to 'planetary life' if the only life-forms in the universe exist on the Earth.

I am well aware that such a way of talking – of the human species as being either 'superior' or 'inferior' to non-human Earthly life – is likely to deeply disturb many humans. There are those who intensely dislike talk of the human species being a 'superior' species. They believe that such a view gives a 'green light' to animal cruelty, to the exploitation of non-human life-forms, and to the continued destruction of the environment. Such humans, quite wrongly in my view, seem to believe that *it is only if* the human species sees itself as not 'superior' to other life-forms that it can act in a respectful way to those life-forms, and to the environment of the Earth as a whole. This last sentence itself raises a very significant issue: there is a difference, and possibly a very important difference, between the way that the human species conceptualises its relationship between itself and the rest of life on Earth, and the actual nature of the relationship between the human species and the rest of life on Earth. The former changes though time; the latter is unchanging. The human species can 'see itself' as not superior, and yet in actuality be superior.

There are others who dislike talk of the human species being 'superior' simply because they believe that such a view is contravened by science. If the evolution of life is all about random mutations, and the organisms which are the 'fittest' (adapt to the environment, greatest offspring) surviving, then, these humans believe, there is no space for a 'superior' species at the top of a hierarchy; there are just species. The truth, it seems to me, is that we actually understand very little (compared to all that there is to possibly know) about either evolution or the nature of the universe; so, such a 'scientific' rejection of superiority should itself be swiftly rejected.[3]

There are also those who intensely dislike talk of the human species being an 'inferior' species. This is typically because such humans strongly believe that the human species is a 'superior' species – unique in its rationality, its capacity for language, its culture, its morality, its spirituality, its consciousness, or some other 'superior' human attribute. The view that the human species is obviously 'superior' is enshrined in many religions – the human species is seen as the only life-form on the Earth which has a special relationship with God. On this view the

_____

[3] For more on this see Chapter Two of: *An Evolutionary Perspective on the Relationship Between Humans and Their Surroundings: Geoengineering, the Purpose of Life & the Nature of the Universe* (2012).

nature of human superiority can be cashed out in many ways, but it is clear that whichever route one takes there is a hierarchy with the human species at its zenith.

There are two different issues which should be made clear: 'superiority' and 'place in the evolutionary process'. There is an increasing tendency within certain religions to accept that the human species evolved through a gradual process of evolution, but to hold that this is compatible with the view that the human species has a position of superiority; this is due to the special place that the human species has in the evolutionary process (a process which was 'designed' by the creator of the process/God). One can also be non-religious and come to this conclusion (that the human species has a position of superiority due to its special place in the evolutionary process); one can believe there was no crea-tor/God, but that there is directionality in the evolution of both life on Earth, and the wider cosmos, directionality which 'aims' towards the human species.

However, there are those who divorce the two issues ('superiority' and 'place in the evolutionary process'). At one extreme are those religious humans who reject evolution and hold that the human species is superior because it was directly created by God. At the other extreme are non-religious 'philosophers/scientists' who believe in evolution but reject the view that the human species has a special 'place in the evolutionary process'; yet these humans hold that the human species is obviously superior, this is because the human species is seen as the unique possessor of any one of a diverse range of attributes – consciousness, a soul, rationality, language, and so on.[4]

Having made these introductory remarks let us consider the 'inferiority' and 'superiority' views in the next two chapters.

---

[4] I reject this basis for deriving 'human superiority' in Chapter Two of: *Is the Human Species Special?: Why human-induced global warming could be in the interests of life?* (2010).

Chapter 1

Inferiority

In the *Introduction* I outlined the view that the human species is inferior to the rest of life on Earth as follows:

> The human species is related to the rest of life on Earth through its inferiority. As the destroyer of a multitude of other life-forms, as the coloniser of the planet, as the destroyer of ecosystems and habitats, as the bringer forth of another mass extinction of life on Earth, the human species must be seen as inferior to

all other life-forms. The human species is a 'parasite' which the rest of life on Earth would be far better off without.

There is obviously an assumption underlying the link between being 'the destroyer of life-forms' and being 'inferior' to these life-forms. The assumption is that life is a precious and valuable part of the universe, and that, therefore, if one species is the destroyer of an enormous number of life-forms, that this species is bad=an unwanted parasite=inferior to the rest of the 'non-destroying' life-forms.

If the human species is the 'inferior destroyer' then there is clearly a deeply significant/important relationship between the human species and the rest of life on Earth. From the perspective of the rest of life on Earth, it has, through the evolutionary process, given birth to a destroyer, a parasite. In other words, non-human life on Earth has, through the evolutionary process, *brought forth that which can end itself*. This might be putting it slightly too strongly, but if the human species doesn't destroy all life on Earth, then it can at least destroy a great proportion of it and wreak great havoc. If we assume that a state of life is good, that the death and destruction of life-forms is bad, then the bringing forth of the human species, by non-human life on Earth, was clearly a very undesirable event, a terribly unfortunate and unwanted 'accident'.

Now, this view of the human species as 'inferior' to the rest of life on Earth, as the destroyer of life, is clearly only a very recent creation of the human mind. For, it is only in very recent times that the human species has become capable of such feats of destruction. Until recently the human population was relatively low, and the human ability to appropriate the resources of the Earth was similarly relatively low. The scientific and technological revolutions, in tandem with the population explosion, have led to the realisation that the human species can be seen as the destroyer of the rest of life on Earth. For the great majority of human history the human species lacked such destructive abilities; for, such an ability requires an immensely high population and/or the possession of immensely complex technology.

Indeed, the widespread appreciation of the human species as the 'inferior destroyer' seems to only have occurred since the evolution of a related concept – the 'environmental crisis'. It is seemingly the realisation that humans have created what humans call the 'environmental crisis' that has caused many humans to conceive of the human species as the 'inferior destroyers'. What exactly is the 'environmental crisis'? It is a collection of certain 'environmental problems'. What is an 'environmental problem'? Sloep and Dam-Mieras define an 'environmental problem' as follows:

> any change of state in the physical environment which is brought about by human interference with the physical environment, and has effects which society deems unacceptable in the light of its shared norms.[5]

---

[5] Peter B. Sloep and Maris C.E. van Dam-Mieras, 'Science on Environmental Problems', in P. Glasbergen and A. Blowers (eds.) *Environmental Policy in an International Context: Perspectives,* Oxford, Butterworth-Heinmann, 2003, p. 42.

So, it is the "shared norms" of society which gives rise to 'environmental problems', and in turn, gives rise to the 'environmental crisis'. A particular set of physical changes could occur and whether or not these changes constitute an 'environmental crisis' depends on the way that humans think about these changes. The physical changes that humans have initiated are currently very widely thought about/conceptualised solely as 'very bad' – that is why they are widely thought of as leading to a 'crisis' – the 'environmental crisis'. This conceptualisation leads to an inevitable conclusion: as the initiators of the 'crisis' the human species is the 'destroyer' – the 'inferior destroyer'.

This is how I describe this view in *Is the Human Species Special?: Why human-induced global warming could be in the interests of life?* (2010, pp. 50-1):

According to one prominent contemporary view the rest of planetary life would be far better off if the human species were to become extinct! As the human species has spread out over the entire planet one effect has been that many species have become extinct, and unfortunately many more are in grave danger of extinction. The human species has turned natural habitats into 'concrete jungles'; it has initiated mass deforestation and mass agriculture; through its web of trade and transport links it has imported alien species into inappropriate habitats where the result has been the decimation of the native species; and it has released large amounts of oil into the oceans with disastrous effects. Now, many see the threat of human-induced global warming as the final 'nail in the coffin' of other species. According to this view, the human species through its selfish desire to plunder the world's resources in order to have a high standard of living is set to destroy a multitude of species, and possibly itself too.

So, if one has seen a lot of nature documentaries one will probably have heard many commentators assert that if the human species were to become extinct this would be great news for the rest of life on Earth. According to this currently popular view if the human species were to become extinct the rest of the species on the planet would be saved from our destructive influence. The advocates of this view believe that a couple of millennia after the extinction of the human species the biological diversity of the Earth would be vastly higher; life would supposedly be flourishing in the absence of the destructive humans. This view is grounded in what has happened in the past. In the past when there have been mass extinctions of life on Earth it *has* been the case that after a long period of time life has recovered; after a long enough period of time the biological diversity of the Earth has become just as rich as it was before the mass extinction. However, as I am sure you will appreciate, one cannot always use the past as a guide to the future.

I have recently noticed various places where this widespread contemporary view, of humanity as the 'destroyer' which the rest of life on Earth would be far better off without, has seeped into films, television and the media. On the following pages I present numerous examples of this view.

1   Film: 'The Day the Earth Stood Still' (2008)

Description:

"After an alien visitor lands in Central Park, a professor makes the drastic decision to help him escape from US military custody. When the visitor sees the destruction man has wreaked on the planet, he makes the decision to destroy mankind. Oops."

(TV Guide: *Latest7,* 14-20 February 2012, p. 35)

2   Film: 'The 11th Hour' (2008)

Description:

"Environmental documentary 11th HOUR resides at the polar opposite of escapist summer fare, its mission to firmly confront viewers about the indelible human footprint that humans have left on this planet, and the catastrophic effects of environmental neglect and abuse."

http://astore.amazon.com/resourcesforlife/detail/B00005JPXA/

[accessed 24 February 2012]

3   Film: 'An Inconvenient Truth' (2006)

Description:

"Director Davis Guggenheim eloquently weaves the science of global warming with Al Gore's personal history and lifelong commitment to reversing the effects of global climate change in the most talked-about documentary of the year. An audience and critical favorite, An Inconvenient Truth makes the compelling case that global warming is real, man-made, and its effects will be cataclysmic if we don't act now."

http://astore.amazon.com/resourcesforlife/detail/B000ICL3KG/

[accessed 24 February 2012]

4 Film: 'The Yes Men Fix the World' (2009)

Description:

"This is a screwball true story about two gonzo political activists who, posing as top executives of giant corporations, lie their way into big business conferences and pull off the world's most outrageous pranks. From New Orleans to India to New York City, armed with little more than cheap thrift-store suits, the Yes Men squeeze raucous comedy out of all the ways that corporate greed is destroying the planet."

http://www.grinningplanet.com/6001/environmental-movies.htm

[accessed 24 February 2012]

5   Film: 'The Day After Tomorrow' (2004)

Description:

"A climatologist tries to figure out a way to save the world from abrupt global warming. He must get to his young son in New York, which is being taken over by a new ice age."

http://www.imdb.com/title/tt0319262/

[accessed 24 February 2012]

6   TV: 'State of the Planet' (2000)

Sir David Attenborough

"It seems that we'll have to make further changes in our behaviour and attitude if we're not to inflict lasting damage on the other animals and plants with which we share this planet. We ourselves as a species may well survive come what may... The future of life on Earth depends on our ability to take action. Many individuals are doing what they can but real success can only come if there is a change in our societies and our economics and in our politics. I have been lucky in my lifetime to see some of the greatest spectacles that the natural world has to offer, surely we have a responsibility to leave future generations a planet that is healthy and habitable by all species."

BBC Video Tape (2000). Stereo BBCV 7097.

7   TV: 'Earth: The Power of the Planet' (2007)

Professor Iain Stewart

Description 1:

"The air we breathe, the oceans we sail, the ice we marvel at and the volcanoes we dread: over the course of 4.6 billion years these elements have created a planet capable of sustaining a vast number of complex life-forms. In Earth: The Power of the Planet, Dr Iain Stewart travels to some of the globe's most breathtaking locations to explain how Earth works. He also wants us to understand just how privileged we are to be here. The Earth has had a number of lucky breaks on the way to becoming a life-giving planet. Are humans in danger of reversing that good fortune?"

http://uktv.co.uk/eden/item/aid/610587

[accessed 24 February 2012]

Description 2:

"In each episode, geologist Dr. Iain Stewart explains the effects and importance of a specific force of nature, such as wind or volcanism. He also examines the various ways in which it shapes planet earth itself and influences life on it, often in conjunction with other natural forces, and sometimes with lifeforms, as in the 'apocalyptically' grave case of global warming."

http://www.imdb.com/title/tt1145500/

[accessed 24 February 2012]

8   TV: 'Are We Changing Planet Earth?' (2006)

Sir David Attenborough

"We are heading for a great worsening of the conditions of this planet for life of all kinds and I have no doubt whatsoever of the cause, which is the byproducts of humanity's activities and that therefore we should be curbing them"

(Interview with Sir David Attenborough concerning the above documentary):

http://www.guardian.co.uk/science/blog/2007/jun/25/sirdavidattenboroughonglob

[accessed 24 February 2012]

9   News: 'Time Lapse Satellite Photos Show How Humans Are Destroying The World' (2011)

"It takes a lot to provide for 7 billion humans. Mankind is destroying rainforests, draining marshes and drilling into mountains to provide timber, water, coal and other resources. Some of this destruction has been captured in before and after satellite photos."

http://www.businessinsider.com/satellite-photos-destroying-the-world-2011-3

[accessed 25 February 2012]

10 Magazine: *New Internationalist* 'Life' (2005)

"Life on earth first evolved in the oceans over 2.5 billion years ago. Perhaps half a million years ago, one species of primate became more and more successful, and humanity spread throughout the world. By 10,000 years ago we were domesticating plants and animals; and by the 20th century our high-energy technologies and productive activities meant we were capable of the total transformation of ecosystems, something unprecedented in history.

The number of species threatened with extinction is a clear indicator of the state of the world's ecosystems. Extinction means the death of birth. Five mass extinctions have happened in the past 500 million years. The sixth and greatest extinction in the history of our planet is happening today. It is almost entirely due to human activity, and is faster than any in history: we are losing species at a rate of up to 1,000 times the natural rate of extinction. Between a third and a half of terrestrial species are expected to die out over the next two centuries if current trends continue unchecked.

Humanity's threats to biodiversity are manifold, from habitat loss to destruction of grasslands and forests, from overfishing, pollution and contamination to global climate change. The inter-relatedness of ecosystems means that a small loss in one area can affect many other species around it: for example, the decline of the honeybee leaves many fruit crops and flowers unpollinated. For in nature, diversity breeds diversity: trees in turn provide homes and food for birds, insects, other plants and animals and fungi."

Issue 378   2005

http://www.newint.org/features/2005/05/01/ecosystems-life

[Accessed 2 March 2012]

It is clear from the above that the human species is currently quite widely viewed as the 'destroyer', even as a 'parasite', and that the rest of life on Earth would be much better off if it were free of our destructive influence. This is a very widespread view. How often have you seen a film, or a television programme, which portrays the human species as the 'saviour' of life on Earth, rather than as the destroyer? I would be surprised if you have seen a single film/programme on this theme.

Indeed, such a way of thinking – of humans as the destroyers – is contemporarily so widely ingrained and propagated, that one might even have trouble accepting the possibility that the human species could actually be the most precious and valued part of life on Earth, because it is the saviour of life on Earth. In other words, from the perspective of the rest of life on Earth, the human species is not the destroyer, it is the saviour. Let us now turn to this possibility.

Chapter 2

Superiority

In the previous chapter we explored the very widespread contemporary view that the human species is the 'inferior destroyer' which the rest of life on Earth would be far better off without. This view is exemplified in the following belief:

> The lesson we need to learn urgently is this: we cannot do without the rest of the planet's biodiversity, but it can do very well without us.[6]

[6] *New Internationalist* 'Life', Issue 378, 2005: http://www.newint.org/features/2005/05/01/ecosystems-life [Accessed 2 March 2012]

In this chapter my aim is to outline a view which violently clashes with the above belief. According to the 'superiority' view life on Earth, in contradiction to the above quote, most definitely *cannot* "do very well without us".

In the *Introduction* I outlined the view that the human species is superior to the rest of life on Earth as follows:

The human species is related to the rest of life on Earth through its superiority. There is a hierarchy of life and the human species is located at its zenith. The human species is the most precious/valuable/important part of life on Earth.

In the *Introduction* I also noted that many humans, despite not believing that the evolutionary process 'aims' for the human species, still consider it to be 'obvious' that the human species is the most important part of life on Earth. This is because they believe that the human species is the unique possessor of any one of a diverse range of attributes – consciousness, a soul, rationality, language...the list goes on and on. I also noted in the *Introduction* that I reject this basis for ascribing 'human superiority'.

In *Is the Human Species Special?: Why human-induced global warming could be in the interests of life?,* the basis of rejection that I focus on is twofold. Firstly, whichever 'unique' human attribute one cares to choose, there are very good reasons to believe that it is not uniquely human (there are at least some non-human Earthly life-forms which also have the attribute). Secondly (and particularly if one is not convinced by the first basis of rejection), there is a sense in which all 'species' have 'unique' attributes, and there is no basis for saying that unique human attributes are 'superior' to the unique attributes of non-human life-forms (unless one grounds this belief in a view according to which the unique human attributes have been 'aimed at' through the evolutionary progression of life – these attributes being the zenith of the evolutionary progression of life).

Here I would like to focus on another aspect of why one should reject this basis for ascribing 'human superiority'. Humans can, of course, come up with an almost endless list of supposedly 'unique attributes' which results in them placing themselves in a position of superiority above the rest of life on

Earth. However, this is really not of much interest to us. What we are concerned with is not 'self-image'. We are concerned with the possible nature of *a relationship* – the relationship between the human species and the rest of life on Earth. In particular, we are interested in the nature of this relationship *from the perspective of non-human planetary life*. From the perspective of 'the rest' of life on Earth is there anything about the human species which would cause the human species to be bolstered into a position of superiority? This is the crucial point.

Would the rest of life on Earth be in a state of celebration simply because the Earth evolved a species – the human species – which could communicate via language (whereas the rest of life, it is hypothesised, only communicates via 'non-language')? I really don't see why, even if this was true, that in-itself it would be a reason for non-human life to want to elevate the human species to a position of superiority.

Would the rest of life on Earth be in a state of celebration simply because the Earth evolved a species – the human species – which has awareness (whereas the rest of life, it is hypothesised, is wholly unaware)? I really don't see why, even if this was true (and it seems exceedingly untrue), that in-itself it would be a reason for non-human life to want to elevate the human species to a position of superiority.

And so it goes on, plug in any attribute you like, 'soul', 'rationality', 'culture'. In themselves, why would such attributes, from the perspective of non-human life-forms, be a reason for them to wish to elevate the human species to a position of 'superiority'? If there is a zenith, if there is a hierarchy with the human species at the top, we need a blindingly obvious reason why this is so. We shouldn't be grasping around for various diverse attributes – maybe 'tool use', maybe 'awareness', maybe a 'soul', maybe 'language', maybe 'rationality', maybe 'culture'! Such grasping just undermines the idea that there is a hierarchy with the human species at the zenith.

So, it is clear that I reject this basis for ascribing 'human superiority' (and I believe that you should reject it too). Yet, it is seemingly blindingly obvious that there is a hierarchy, and that the human species is at its zenith. And this is obvious when we consider not human 'self-image' – the desire of humans to find an attribute which elevates themselves above the 'animals' – but the *relation-*

ship between non-human Earthly life-forms and the human species. This is because the human species is the saviour of these life-forms.

Despite the contemporary pervasiveness of the view that the human species is the 'destroyer' of life on Earth, it is likely that you will have come across the idea that the human species could actually be the saviour of life on Earth. Recall Noah's Ark. The human species saves two of every life-form that exists on the Earth from a great flood. In the absence of the human species these life-forms would have perished in the flood. In this conceptualisation of the relationship between the human species and their surroundings the human species is the saviour of life on Earth. Through the 'technological' knowledge which had been accumulated over a great deal of time, particular humans, such as Noah, were able to construct the Ark in order to save the rest of life on Earth. By taking two of each animal the human species was enabling a long and prosperous future for life on Earth; over time, through reproduction, the population levels could be restored to their pre-flood levels.

The 'Noah's Ark conceptualisation' is limited to events on the Earth itself. There is a flood on the Earth, and the human species, through its techno-logical ability, is able to construct an Ark to save all of the life-forms that exist on the Earth; this enables the Earth to be repopulated when the flood has subsided. A more recent conceptualisation of the human species as saviour of life on Earth takes on more cosmic proportions. It has been suggested by Terence McKenna that:

the world soul is the thing that wants to live...[it] may actually sense the finite life of the sun, and it may be trying to build a lifeboat for itself to cross to another star. How in the world can you cross to another star when the only material available to you is protoplasm? Well it may take fifty million years, but there are strategies. They have to do with genetic languages, and with developing a creature who deals with matter through abstraction and analysis, eventually creating technology."[7]

---

[7] McKenna, Terence, R. Abraham, & R. Sheldrake, *Chaos, Creativity and Cosmic Consciousness*, (Rochester: Park Street Press, 2001), pp. 69-70.

According to this view life is a particularly precious part of the universe (the 'world soul') and in order to survive, because of the future death of the Sun, it needs to leave the Earth. The death of the Sun can be compared to the 'great flood'. Instead of an Ark being required, what is required in this conceptualisation is another technological creation – a spaceship (a "lifeboat") which can transport lifeforms off the Earth. As the part of life on Earth which has become technological, the human species has to be the creator of such a spaceship, and the human species is therefore the saviour of life on Earth.

It is worth briefly considering what it means for the human species to be 'the saviour of life on Earth'. In the *Introduction* (pp. 20-22) I referred to 'planetary life' and the 'totality of *non-human*

Earthly life' ('planetary life' minus humans). These conceptualisations/terms are useful because it is natural for 'species' to go extinct. Indeed, the extinction of species is a process which has been ongoing since the non-living universe brought forth 'planetary life'. So, to say that the human species is the saviour of life on Earth is really to say that the human species is the saviour of 'non-human Earthly life' (recall that this is a single entity, *not* lots of individual life-forms). In other words, it isn't realistic to expect the human species to save every single life-form, or every single 'species', that exists (and recall that 'species' boundaries could simply be human conceptualisations, so to talk of saving 'every species' could, strictly speaking, be meaningless). If the human species manages to save itself and a large-part (or even a small part) of 'non-human

Earthly life', from what would be, in the absence of human technology, death, then the human species is 'the saviour of life on Earth'.

There is a close similarity between McKenna's assertion and the view that I outline in *Is the Human Species Special?: Why human-induced global warming could be in the interests of life?* In assessing the contemporarily fashionable 'inferior destroyer' view I state (2010, p. 51):

My hope is to open you to the idea that this contemporarily fashionable view is wrong. The root of its wrongness is that it does not account for the fact that the Earth and the Sun are ageing entities. Furthermore, I contend that planetary life has been striving to bring the human species into existence since it first arose. So, if the human species were to become extinct now it would *not* be great news for planetary life; it would be an utter disaster.

My view of human superiority is similar to McKenna's view because both views are grounded in the realisation that the solar system is an evolving entity and that the Sun – the enabler of life on Earth – will, in the future, cease to exist. Once one realises this then it is easy to see the human species, as the bringers forth of the technology which can save life on Earth from future extinction, as the most precious life-form on the planet. This 'preciousness' is not generated from the perspective of humans themselves, it is generated from the perspective of all life on Earth, and even from the perspective of the entire universe. Through their technological abilities and creations (whether it is Noah's Ark, McKenna's lifeboat, or the range of technologies I outline below) the human species would be 'viewed' as the 'saviour' by all of the diverse life-forms which get saved.

In a sense, there is nothing particularly controversial about McKenna's view. It is fairly widely accepted that in the future the Sun will expire (if one denied this and asserted that the Sun will exist forever, one would not be taken too seriously). From this it straightforwardly follows that in the future, if the life that has arisen on the Earth is to survive, it needs to be saved by technology. Life on Earth, through bringing forth the human species, has brought forth the saviour that it requires. Could this be a coincidence? Or could it be an outcome which was striven for. You will probably have already realised that both McKenna and I favour the latter view; we don't find the idea that such a bringing forth of technology was a 'coincidence' to be a convincing idea.

There is scope here for divergent opinions, after all, we are talking about the fundamental nature of the universe and the way that this nature causes the universe to gradually evolve and change through time. I believe that the fundamental nature of the universe is 'feeling' and that these feelings are responsible for the way that the universe evolves through time.[8] The universe (= an aggregate of lots

---

[8] I make the philosophical case for such a view (after exploring existing paradigms such as 'materialism', 'panpsychism', 'panexperientialism' and 'pansensism') in *An Evolutionary Perspective on the Relationship Between Humans and Their Surroundings: Geoengineering, the Purpose of Life & the Nature of the Universe* (2012).

of individual feelings) is always seeking to move to a higher state of feeling. This 'seeking' is what causes life to arise wherever possible (the living is a higher/better state of feeling than the non-living), it is also what gives rise to directionality in biological and cultural evolution. From this perspective, the human species, as the bringers forth of technology, as the zenith of the evolutionary progression of life on Earth, is the highest/best state of feeling on the Earth. To say that the human species was striven for by the non-human life-forms that brought the human species into existence is not to say that these life-forms had a meeting and discussed such an objective, or anything of this kind. These life-forms, as part of the feeling universe, were simply seeking to move to a higher state of feeling.

Humans, as part of the feeling universe, are also pervaded with feelings throughout every part of their bodies. There is a natural instinct within humans to avoid bad feelings and to move to/stay in states of good feelings. The feeling of pain is generally thought of as a feeling which is best avoided if possible; replacing it with a feeling of bliss would generally be an outcome which most humans seek. In this way, by seeking to move to a higher/better state of feeling, humans act in certain ways and thereby cause human culture to evolve in a certain direction. Exploring/creating/bringing forth technology, these are all things which make humans feel good. The feeling universe pervades everything, and its objectives get fulfilled through feelings.

The feeling universe seems to be very similar to the view of the universe envisioned by the philosopher Arthur Schopenhauer who claimed that:

Everything presses and pushes towards existence, if possible organic existence, i.e. life, and then to the highest possible degree thereof.[9]

What is doing this "pressing and pushing"? Schopenhauer describes the nature of the universe as 'blind will'. We can, it seems to me, fruitfully think of this 'blind will' as feeling states seeking to reach a higher/better state of feeling.

---

[9] Schopenhauer, Arthur, *The World as Will and Representation*, Volume II, Trans. E. F. J. Payne, (New York: Dover Publications, 1958), p. 350.

There is a long-standing spiritual tradition according to which humans seek to 'live in accordance with their feelings'. Let me comment briefly on this. If the universe in its entirety is a feeling universe, then it seems to me that the vast majority of movements in the universe occur almost automatically. For example, atom A1 likes the feeling of atom A2, and vice versa, so A1 and A2 come together and form a molecule. These feelings/movements underpin the evolution of the universe. Now, in certain parts of the universe things seem to be a little more complex than these automatic movements. I have in mind those parts of the universe which think (and possibly *just* those parts of the universe which are aware of their thoughts); and it is plausible that these parts of the universe only exist in brains.

Where there is thinking, the movements of the universe seem to not be automatic. Thinking can *prevent* a particular part of the universe from moving to a higher state of feeling. Thinking is like a 'prevention device' which can stop the normal course of events from occurring. Most parts of the universe simply 'automatically' move into the best state of feeling possible. But, if there is thought, then such a movement can be blocked. In other words, 'thinkers' can be their own worst enemy. This is why it is important to be in tune with one's feelings. If one is 'in tune' in this way one can almost effort-lessly move to an optimal state of feeling; one simply lets the universe do its thing within one; one lets the universe naturally move to the highest/best state of feeling. If one is not 'in tune' with one's feelings then one can make decisions which result in such a natural movement being blocked; one can thereby end up living a less happy life than would otherwise be the case. As the vast majority of humans consciously, or unconsciously, loosely make decisions which are in accordance with their feelings, the overall outcome is that human culture evolves in the direction that is desired by the feeling universe as a whole entity. I say 'loosely' because I am sure there is vast scope for the vast majority of humans to live even closer to the feelings which are within them, and thereby to live more fulfilling lives.

I might seem to have diverged from the theme of this chapter, which is the view that the human species is superior to the rest of life on Earth. However, if one is to claim that the human species is the zenith of the evolutionary progression of life on Earth, that the bringing forth of technology was not a 'coincidence', then one needs to give an account of how this can be so, and of how this plays out in the life of individual humans. I initially sought to do this in *Is the Human Species Special?: Why human-induced global warming could be in the interests of life*. I hope that here I have added usefully to the view outlined there.

So, to be clear, my claim is that the human species is the most precious/valuable/important part of life on Earth because it is the bringer forth of technology. As we live in a 'feeling universe' which achieves its aims through attempting to move to the highest/best state of feeling possible, another way of saying this is: *the human species is the most precious/valuable/important part of life on Earth because it is the highest state of feeling on the Earth.*

Now, why exactly is technology so important? Why does the human species, as the bringer forth of technology, equate to the highest state of feeling on the Earth? Recall that earlier I claimed that:

In a sense, there is nothing particularly controversial about McKenna's view. It is fairly widely accepted that in the future the Sun will expire (if one denied this and asserted that the Sun will exist forever, one would not be taken too seriously). From this it straightforwardly follows that in the future, if the life that has arisen on the Earth is to survive, it needs to be saved by technology.

It does seem obvious to me that this is right. That the human species, via its technology, is the only hope that life on Earth has of surviving. And I believe that when we look at Mckenna's view from the perspective of the 'feeling universe' that we can make sense of how the non-human life-forms that preceded the human species brought forth their saviour.

However, whilst "this is right", we are here, apparently, talking about the very distant future. Mckenna's view focuses on the point in the future when the Sun has heated up immensely compared to today and when it finally expires. There are two more aspects relating to technology being the saviour of life on Earth which I would like to explore. Firstly, I believe that there are numerous ways in which technology can be utilised in order to save life on Earth; simply talking of an 'Ark', or of a "lifeboat", misses the whole range of benefits that technology brings to life on Earth. Secondly, I would like to comment on the idea (outlined in *Is the Human Species Special?: Why human-induced global warming could be in the interests of life?* and in *An Evolutionary Perspective on the Relationship Between Humans and Their Surroundings: Geoengineering, the Purpose of Life & the Nature of the Universe)* that the environmental crisis/human-induced global warming are positive events which indicate that the human species is fulfilling its role as the saviour of life on Earth.

So, what are the numerous ways in which technology can be utilised in order to save life on Earth? Let me start with the exceedingly obvious: meteor strike. There has recently been renewed concern that a massive meteor is on a collision course to hit the Earth in the not too distant future. Groups of humans are, at this present moment, working hard to construct the technologies which can either deflect or destroy such incoming meteors. If these technologies are successfully developed and utilised then the human species, by deflecting/destroying that which has the potential to destroy life on Earth, is clearly acting so as to be the saviour of life on Earth. Of this there can be no doubt; the human species would be the technological saviour of life on Earth. Through bringing forth the human species life on Earth has given birth to a set of protective armour in order to help to ensure its future survival.

How else can technology be utilised in order to save life on Earth? Well, there are a range of possibilities, some a little more far-fetched and implausible than others. Firstly, there are threats to the continued existence of life on Earth which arise from the operations of the non-living operations of the Earth. For example, it is likely that in the future there will be a massive supervolcano explosion, and it is at least plausible that such an explosion could wipe out most, if not all, of the life-forms on the Earth. This eventuality could be avoided if the human species was able to construct a large 'building' with an artificial atmosphere (a kind of stationary Ark, or even something which circulates in the atmosphere) which is self-propagating, isolated from the atmosphere and workings of the rest of the Earth, and contains a diverse range of habitats. If the life-forms of the Earth existed within such a technological creation then they could survive the change of planetary conditions brought about by the supervolcano explosion. Once again, the human species is the technological saviour of life on Earth.

Another possible threat, which is hard to assess for its plausibility, is that life on Earth could be invaded by 'aliens' which seek to destroy life on Earth. If life on Earth is technologically prepared, through the human species, then it might be able to defend itself. Needless to say, if this situation was to pertain, and the human technology was successful, then the rest of life on Earth would be 'grateful' to its saviour.

Now, I hope you can see the numerous ways in which it is obvious that life on Earth benefits from becoming technological; the numerous ways in which the human species is able to act as the saviour of life on Earth.

Let me now turn to my belief that the environmental crisis/human-induced global warming are positive events which indicate that the human species is fulfilling its role as the saviour of life on Earth. The 'inferior destroyer' view focuses solely on the negative aspects of technology; it doesn't appreciate that these effects are massively outweighed by the positive aspects of technology.

What is the 'environmental crisis'? At its simplest this term refers to the fact that humans have utilised a lot of the resources of the Earth, and in doing so have made changes to the biosphere of the planet which are potentially worrying. From the perspective of the 'feeling universe' we can see that this outcome was inevitable. Most humans in the past, and today, simply do what increases their state of feeling to higher/better states. The German Romantic Friedrich Hölderlin saw this clearly:

> Why can they [humans] not live contented like the beasts of the field? he asks: and replies that this would be as unnatural in man, as in animals the tricks, or arts, man trains them to perform. Thus he establishes that the arts of man are natural to man. Culture, then, derives from nature; and the impulse to it is the characteristic which distinguishes man from the rest of creation."[10]

---

[10] Peacock, Ronald, *Hölderlin,* London, Methuen & Co. Ltd, 1938, p. 36.

The 17th century philosopher Baruch Spinoza also saw that this was so. He asserted that humans simply cannot deprive themselves of those things which they judge to be the most conducive to their own welfare (those things which 'optimise' their feeling states). This is a principle which is:

inscribed so firmly in the human breast [that it constitutes an] immutable [truth that] nobody [can] ignore. [11]

So, I am suggesting that the utilisation of the Earth's resources by the human species is not bad. It is simply the outcome of humans acting on the

---

[11] Baruch Spinoza, *Tractatus Theologico-Politicus* [1670], Emilia Giancotti Boscherini (Ed.), (Torino, 1972), I, p. 472.

feelings which have been endowed to them by the universe as the universe seeks to move to a higher state of feeling. It is only by utilising the Earth's resources on a massive scale that the understanding could be attained which enables life on Earth to give birth to its protective technological armour. Recall McKenna's claim that the 'aim' of life is:

developing a creature who deals with matter through abstraction and analysis, eventually creating technology

If this is the aim of life, if the zenith of the evolutionary progression of life on Earth is the bringing forth of a 'bringer-forth of technology', then we can see that the human species, as the 'bringer-forth' of technology, is the zenith of the evolutionary progression of life on Earth.

There is no doubt that the massive utilisation of planetary resources by the human species has resulted in 'worrying' changes; it is these changes that constitute the 'environmental crisis'. However, overall the changes are a part of a positive event, they are part of the birthing process which is occurring as life on Earth develops its protective armour. In other words, the 'environmental crisis' is a good thing. Now, if you were to take the last sentence in isolation from all that has gone before, then it would probably sound wildly implausible, obviously false, or even mildly offensive. However, given all that has gone before, I hope you can see that it is simply obviously true.

I am not claiming that many of the changes that the human species have made to the planet are not things that we should be concerned about. Many of the changes have, when considered in isolation, been quite terrible. I'm here thinking of changes such as the suffering caused by chemical leaks, nuclear explosions, oil leaks, and pollution of all kinds. It is just that when we consider these events from the perspective of the wider 'birthing process' which is presently occurring on the planet – life on Earth developing its technological armour – then these terrible events need to be seen as worth the pain. I'm not a woman, but I can imagine that the 'birthing process' whilst entailing considerable pain, is often looked back on as a desirable event overall (and is even something which is aimed for again in the future – the pain was worth the gain). As with a woman, so for life on Earth. And just as a woman can look back at the pain and see that is was worthwhile, I'm suggesting that this will be the case in the future for the human species and life on Earth as a whole. It is a long 'birthing process', but when the technological armour has been fully developed, an era of harmony and sustainability can exist.

We currently live in the midst of a painful birthing process, there is suffering, there is pain, humans and other life-forms are subjected to such pain/suffering at the hands of technology ever day. We face great challenges in bringing this process to a successful conclusion. In particular, we face the spectre of global warming. Complex life-forms need the temperature of the atmosphere to be in a particular range in order to survive, if it shoots upwards then all is lost.

In my previous writings I have made the case that the human species needs, *in the near future*, to technologically regulate the temperature of the Earth's atmosphere. It is actually widely accepted that *in the distant future* the Sun will be sending much more energy to the Earth than it presently does, and that the planet will then be too hot for almost all, if not all, life-forms to exist. That is, *unless* those life-forms are technologically controlling the temperature of the Earth's atmosphere.

My belief, that life needs such technological control of the atmosphere *in the near future*, is more controversial. This might be partially because most humans haven't considered all of the various factors which I am seeking to bring together in my recent writings on the subject. The 'near future' view is grounded in the belief that, in accordance with Gaia

Theory, life on Earth, in tandem with non-living components of the biosphere, has been regulating the temperature of the biosphere in order to keep it in a range which can sustain complex life. The problem is that this homeostatic regulatory capacity has been weakening for some time (due to the increasing output of the Sun), and it has been further perturbed by the release of carbon dioxide from its underground storage areas by the human species. This is what Sir James Lovelock has to say on the matter:

If our planetary temperature depended only on the abiological constraints set by the sun's output and the heat balance of the Earth's atmosphere and surface, then... all life would have been eliminated.[12]

[Gaia] is old and has not very long to live. As the sun grows ever hotter it will, in Gaia's terms, soon become too hot for animals and plants and many of the microbial forms of life.[13]

only for a brief period in the Earth's history was the sun's warmth ideal for life, and that was about two billion years ago. Before this it was too cold for comfort and afterwards it

[12] Lovelock, J., 2000. *Gaia: A new look at life on Earth.* Oxford: Oxford University Press, p. 20.
[13] Lovelock, J., 2006. *The Revenge of Gaia.* London: Penguin Books Ltd. p. 46.

has progressively grown too hot... The sun is already too hot for comfort.[14]

In short, the main threat to life on Earth in the future is the increasing output of the Sun. This threat can only be countered by the technological regulation of the temperature of the Earth's atmosphere by that part of life which has become technological – the human species. I have suggested that the recognition of, and concern about, human-induced global warming, might actually be the stimulus which causes the human species to develop a large part of the technological armour (the techno-

---

[14] Lovelock, J., 2006. *The Revenge of Gaia*. London: Penguin Books Ltd. pp. 44-5.

logical regulation of the atmosphere) which life on Earth so badly needs.[15]

From the perspective of the terminology I have been using here, this regulation can be seen as the major component of the 'birthing process' which is currently occurring on the planet. When the temperature of the atmosphere is successfully being technologically regulated the birthing process will be near its conclusion.

Achieving such a successful birth will not be an easy or pain-free journey. There are dangers and obstacles to be overcome. However, the more prepared we are the easier the birth will be.

---

[15] For more on this see my: *Is the Human Species Special?: Why human-induced global warming could be in the interests of life?* (2010) and *An Evolutionary Perspective on the Relationship Between Humans and Their Surroundings: Geoengineering, the Purpose of Life & the Nature of the Universe* (2012).

I want to stress that there are a range of dangers that we face in the near future. I wouldn't want you to finish reading this book with the impression that everything is rosy, that there are no environmental concerns for one to be worried about. It is true that I have described the environmental crisis and human-induced global warming as good/positive events, but I've also stressed that they are part of a painful birthing process which entails a range of dangers.

The birthing process concludes when the temperature of the atmosphere is being successfully technologically regulated, and the range of other technological protections that I have described above are successfully developed. The technological armour is primarily concerned with the atmosphere of the planet – controlling its temperature and preventing massive meteors from entering it. On the surface of the Earth there are a plethora of environmental concerns which humans need to be very concerned about, and for which there is seemingly no obvious techno-fix.

One shouldn't believe that technology is the answer/solution for everything. The birthing process that I have been describing operates for the interests of life on Earth, and the wider cosmos. Its outcome is simply to protect life on Earth through developing technological armour. It isn't a birthing process which is focused on bringing sustainability to human society across the planet. There are a great number of problems which humans face in the immediate future if they are to attain a sustainable, peaceful and harmonious future. These problems need to be faced up to and various solutions need to be considered; sometimes technology might be part of the solution, and sometimes technology might have no role to play whatsoever. Some of the problems that I have in mind are diminishing fresh water supplies, eroding top soil levels, an escalating human population level, social inequality, excessive resource use per head combined with diminishing resources, and excessive waste.

There are a range of environmental problems that we face, and actions need to be taken to address these problems. A sustainable and desirable future human existence on the planet requires such environmentally friendly actions to be taken. The issue which needs to be addressed is the question of which actions are required to successfully resolve particular problems.

I have claimed that we live in the midst of a technological birthing process, and that this process will continue until a successful birth has been delivered. The birth cannot be aborted because humans, as part of the feeling universe, will largely continue to seek to live in accordance with their optimal feeling states (recall the quotes from Hölderlin and Spinoza).

The birth – the technological control of the temperature of the atmosphere – is not something which is negotiable. So, let us prepare for the oncoming birth, and make it as smooth as possible. The birthing process is inherently painful but the pain, the suffering, both to humans and to non-human life-forms, can be reduced. As the bringers forth of such pain/suffering, in order to be the saviours of life on Earth, the human species is 'superior' to the rest of life on Earth. This curious mix of suffering and saviour caused Hölderlin to characterise the human species as a "sour grape" which was brought forth to fulfil a cosmic purpose:

What is man? – so I might begin; how does it happen that the world contains such a thing, which ferments like a chaos or moulders like a rotten tree, and never grows to ripeness? How can Nature tolerate this sour grape among her sweet clusters?"[16]

---

[16] Friedrich Hölderlin , 'Hyperion', in Eric L. Santner (ed.), *Hyperion and Selected Poems,* New York, Continuum, 1990, p. 35.

For Hölderlin, man is the 'violent' being, whose coming into existence in opposition to the rest of nature was initiated by nature. From the perspective of the 'environmental crisis' we can see that the human species is 'violent' in order to 'save'; it was brought forth into existence in order to be violent=save. The 'opposition' exists because the human species is the zenith of the evolutionary progression of life on Earth = the bringer forth of technology = the initialiser of the birthing process of the technological armour of the planet.

Accepting that this is so does not mean that there aren't a range of environmental problems which we need to deal with on the surface of the Earth. Indeed, the birthing process has inevitably given rise to a number of such problems, and we need a range of technological and non-technological solutions to deal with these problems. The more effectively and urgently we deal with these problems, the less pain and suffering the birthing process will entail.

Chapter 3

Conclusions

We have been considering the relationship between the human species and the rest of life on Earth. I have outlined three possibilities. Firstly, there is no deeply significant and meaningful relationship. Secondly, the human species is related to the rest of life on Earth through its superiority. Thirdly, the human species is related to the rest of life on Earth through its inferiority.

I have also drawn a distinction between a 'relationship' which is something that obviously exists, and a 'deeply significant and meaningful relationship'. I presume that it is fairly likely that you, before you came across this book, believed that there is a deeply significant and meaningful relationship between the human species and the rest of life on Earth. After all, compare tigers with all non-tiger Earthly life-forms, compare trout with all non-trout Earthly life-forms, compare sparrows with all non-sparrow Earthly life-forms. There are obviously relationships between all of these species – tigers, trout and sparrows – and other Earthly life-forms; such as 'predator-prey' relationships and 'resource competition' relationships. However, when one compares, say, the trout species with the totality of non-trout Earthly life, there just doesn't seem to be a deeply meaningful and significant relationship. In order for there to be such a relationship there would need to be something about the trout species which either puts it at the zenith of the evolutionary progression of life on Earth, or makes it 'inferior' to the rest of life on Earth. No such factor seemingly exists.

However, when you compare the human species with the rest of the Earthly life-forms, it might well seem obvious to you that there is some kind of deeper relationship. There is a long tradition of humans 'grasping around' for an attribute which can elevate themselves into a position of 'superiority' above the rest of the life-forms of the Earth. So, you might well believe (or have believed), that the nature of the deeper relationship (the root of human superiority) is that the human species uniquely has a soul, language, mentality, rationality, awareness, culture, tool-using ability, or something else.

I have described this attempted self-elevation as a concentration on 'self-image' and have suggested that we need to reject this approach and instead take the perspective of what is desirable for non-human Earthly life. When we do this, then, I have claimed, it is blindingly obvious that technology is in the interests of life on Earth. This means that the human species, as that part of life on Earth which is the bringer forth of technology, is 'superior' to the rest of life on Earth. The human species is the bringer forth of the technological armour which can ensure the future survival of life on Earth. The human species is the zenith of the evolutionary progression of life on Earth. The human species is the highest state of feeling on the Earth. The human species is the saviour of life on Earth.

In other words, I have suggested that "when you compare the human species with the rest of the Earthly life-forms, it might well seem obvious to you that there is some kind of deeper relationship". And if this is so, I have suggested that your *belief* is correct. However, I have also suggested that the *grounds for your belief* are likely to be wrong or incomplete. For, the grounds for elevating the human species to a position of 'superiority' is not simply that the human species is the unique posses-sor of Attribute X (take your pick), it is that the human species is the technological saviour of life on Earth.

The situation is a little more complex than this. For, I believe that the reason that humans have been 'grasping around' for an 'elevating-making' attribute for so long is that they have an *inner sense* that they *must be superior*, and this inner sense arises precisely because the human species is the bringer forth of technology. In other words, it is the fact that humans are able to transform/mould/utilise the Earth's resources with such aplomb that gives rise to an inner sense of specialness which, when it reaches the level of rationalisation, gets cashed out through the belief that "humans are superior because they possess Attribute X".

In reality, 'human superiority' is not about possessing an attribute, it is about carrying out certain actions – being the enablers of the birthing process which is life on Earth bringing forth its technological armour. Such a birthing process requires the human species to have particular attributes. However, one shouldn't confuse the two. The possession of an attribute in itself (such as an advanced tool-using ability, or a high-level of rationality) is of no use to Earthly life as a whole, and would not propel a species which has such attributes to a position of superiority. However, if such attributes are utilised to initiate the birthing process that I have outlined, then the initiators of that process are propelled to a position of superiority; the initiators become the zenith of the evolutionary progression of life on Earth – the 'superior saviours'.

What of the view that the nature of the deeply significant and meaningful relationship is that the human species is the 'inferior destroyer'. Before you came across this book you might well have believed this. Indeed, you might well have believed that it is the human 'self-image' of 'superiority' which has caused the human species to actually become the 'destroyer'. And there is probably some truth in this. If the human species didn't see itself as 'superior' would it actually have initiated the birthing process which leads to the bringing forth of the Earth's technological armour? I think the answer is 'no'.

In a sense we seem to be puppets in a cosmic show. We have been brought forth by non-human Earthly life in order to be its saviours. This entails us initiating a painful technological birthing process; we need to initiate pain on ourselves (the stress we personally have to endure through living in a technological society), our fellow species members (car crashes, airplane crashes, mechanical accidents, etc.), and the non-human Earthly life-forms which we have been brought forth to save. Suffering and destruction in order to save! And in order to save, we seemingly have to believe that through the 'environmental crisis' and 'human-induced global warming' in particular, that we are the destroyers. It is through such a belief that the final stages of the technological birthing process get played out. Humans – saviours, destroyers (in order to save), puppets in a cosmic show.

So, how do we deal with our place in this cosmic show? There are two seeming implications:

1   The technological birthing process is a painful process. If we fully accept that that it is occurring, and that the birth is inevitable, we might be able to speed it along and thereby reduce the suffering. We could also more effectively allocate the limited resources that we have. Resources can be focused on geoengineering the temperature of the atmosphere, and resources that are currently being used trying to avoid this outcome can be more fruitfully deployed. They can be used for 'adaptation' programmes, and other

pressing environmental and developmental issues which need to be dealt with at the surface of the Earth.

2 As parts of the 'feeling universe' we can seek to be more effective at living 'in tune' with our feelings and thereby effortlessly move to an optimal state of feeling – one that maximises health and happiness. If one is a cosmic puppet at the mercy of the feelings which are flowing through one, one might as well seek to just go with those feelings and be a happy puppet, rather than seek to 'disobey' those feelings through one's thought process and thereby be an unhappy puppet. One should simply let the universe do its thing within one and let the universe naturally move to the highest/best state of feeling.

I hope that the above is as obvious to
you as it is to me.

http://neilpaulcummins.blogspot.com

Other books by the author:

Is the Human Species Special?: Why human-induced global warming could be in the interests of life (2010)

An Evolutionary Perspective on the Relationship Between Humans and Their Surroundings: Geoengineering, the Purpose of Life & the Nature of the Universe (2012)

What Does it Mean to be 'Green'?: Sustainability, Respect & Spirituality (2011)

Should I be a Vegetarian? : A personal reflection on meat-eating, vegetarianism and veganism (2011)

How Much of Man is Natural? : Two versions of the international prize-winning essay (2011)

The Purpose of the Environmental Crisis : *A Reinterpretation of Hölderlin's Philosophy* (2011)

What is the Problem of Consciousness? :
Materialism, Awareness & What-it-is-likeness
(2011)

Books about the author:

'Human Specialness': The Historical Dimension &
the Historicisation of Humanity. Peter Xavier
Price (2012)

www.ingramcontent.com/pod-product-compliance
Lightning Source LLC
Chambersburg PA
CBHW050531280326
41933CB00011B/1550